It's Time to Soar!

JoLynne Whittaker

© 2018 Clarion Call, LLC

Book Author: Jolynne Whittaker
Book Title: IT'S TIME TO SOAR!
All rights reserved. No part of this publication may be reproduced, stored in a retrieval system or transmited in any form or by any means, electronic, mechanical, photocopying, recording or otherwise without the prior permision of the publisher or in accordance with the provisions of the Copyright, Designs and Patents Act 1988 or under the terms of any licence permitting limited copying issued by the Copyright Licensing Angency.

Published by: Clarion Call, LLC for JoLynne Whittaker Ministries

ISBN-10: 0-9991197-1-0

ISBN-13: 978-0-9991197-1-6

IT'S TIME TO *Soar!*

TABLE OF CONTENTS

Introduction..1

1- *Elevation, Defined*..5

2 - *The Critical Role of Obedience*..9

3 - *Purity Is A Weapon Against the Devil*..15

4 - *A Vital Tool for Elevation*..23

5 - *Radical Alignment*..37

6 - *Clarity (Learning to see yourself the way God sees you)*............49

7 - *Release*..57

8 - *Commitment*..63

In Conclusion...69

Introduction

Are you tired of living at your current level? Are you ready to elevate? If so, the book you're holding in your hands, paired with your Bible, can powerfully help you to do so! By the time you're finished with this book and apply all the Biblical principles, you might just become an exceedingly, abundantly, prosperous and elevated individual! I believe that is God's plan for you.

As a former underdog, I am passionate about helping other people to succeed. I know what it is like to be without food and money, and I know what it's like to feel like you are failing in life. That is not the life of victory our Lord Jesus calls us to live!

All throughout God's Word, the Holy Bible, we read of God's desire to prosper those who love Him. As you study out the Bible, it becomes abundantly clear to every reader that the Lord is a benevolent God, a merciful God, and a strong provider. We also glean that our God loves us to succeed in our lives; He desires for us to thrive.

In my best-selling book, *Stepping Into Favor*, I have delved quite deeply into the principles of God's favor, including how to access God's timeless blessings. In this book, *My Time To Soar*, we will be examining the critical elements required for your **elevation,** specifically. You are about to discover the elements I have personally used and helped literally hundreds of others to use, to elevate successfully. Are you ready?!

It is my great pleasure to impart to you what God has revealed to me from His Word, about requirements and preparation for elevation, as you begin to step into your destiny.

I decree and declare: you're about to step into a season that will be Mighty, Memorable, and Major! You're about to Elevate, in Jesus' name!

- JoLynne Whittaker

Chapter 1
Elevation, Defined

As we begin, I'd like to invite you to begin considering this vial question: What does Elevation mean to you? What does it look like?

I've found that different people have different ideas, even different hopes when it comes to their elevation. Some of us imagine simply changing our surroundings or current lifestyle. Others imagine stepping into a place in God where we can slay all the Goliaths that have haunted our bloodline. Some view elevation as the ability to change the trajectory and very story, of their family.

For some, elevation is strictly financial. For others, elevation is goal or dream-oriented. And for still others, elevation is connected to what they believe their Kingdom assignment to be.

I have found three things to be true, regarding elevation: it is personally tailored, it is always connected to the manifestation of God's promises as found in the Bible, and at its highest level and definition, it is related to one's destiny and purpose.

Some people use the terms favor and elevation interchangeably, but favor and elevation are definitely *not* one and the same.

Stepping into the Favor of God is starkly different than positioning yourself for Elevation and then shifting into it.

Favor is blessing, covering, protection, provision, resources, having supernatural overseers to bless and insulate your life and experiences.

Elevation has to do with destiny; it has to do with purpose. And most always, elevation results in, or is connected to, lifestyle.

Elevation is different for everyone, because everyone has a different purpose. What I'll be helping you with in this intensive, is preparing and positioning yourself so that when God looks at you, He can **see** that you are ready for Elevation. Let's begin!

Chapter 2
The critical role of Obedience

How important is full obedience, to the Lord? How large a role does your full submission to Jesus play, when petitioning the Lord for elevation? Well, disobedience in the eyes of the Lord, is an automatic **NO** as regards your elevation. Why? If one cannot obey Him at their current level, it will be highly questionable if not dubious they'll be able to obey at higher elevations. For new levels bring new devils; higher elevations bring higher challenges. As your elevation gets higher, the stakes get higher.

Therefore, your obedience at your current level — *or lack thereof* — is a clear indicator to God, as to what you are ready for and capable of, pertaining to elevation.

There is a **reason** Samuel said **obedience is better than sacrifice.** — *1 Samuel 15:22*

It means more to the Father to see you obey Him, than to have you sow seeds into ground that may never yield a harvest. It means more to the Lord to see you sold out for Jesus and cheerfully obeying Him, than to see you enthusiastically volunteering at a dead church. Obedience is indeed, far better than sacrifice. Somebody with faith needs to say *Amen* to that!

I've seen people declare breakthrough over and over — never knowing that without **all components of obedience** in place, their breakthrough may very well remain well out of reach.

Could this be the reason you have not elevated? Is disobedience blocking you? If so, and you can honestly admit it, know that the Lord is calling you to repentance, today. Your repentance will move you into submission and obedience, which will in turn position you for elevation.

Disobedience is the real reason far too many Christians **do not** get their breakthrough. They pray for it, they declare it, they even prophesy it — but it never comes to pass. Perhaps then they wonder why, when the real questions all along are: *Are you fully obedient to the Lord? When*

He looks at you, does He see a submitted and obedient servant? Disobedience cancels out blessing and elevation.

Now, when Samuel said obedience is better than sacrifice in *1 Samuel 15:22*, he was speaking to the then reigning King Saul. The prophet then went on to announce Saul's demotion as king.

Why? What happened? Hadn't Saul been the Lord's appointed and anointed? Yes, but Saul's disobedience and lack of self correction, canceled out the elevation! Saul's lack of repentance over his own behavior, escorted him right to the sidelines!

Hear me: while it had been prophesied for Saul to receive the elevation to kingship, disobedience demoted him. — *1 Samuel chapters 10-13*

Saul's behavior and decisions caused the Lord to revoke and rescind Saul's elevation. Let's learn from Saul.

Do not allow disobedience to block or prevent your elevation in this season. I believe many people who will read this book, will come out of rebellion and into obedience. I believe the Lord is speaking to people right now!

When you come into obedience according to the Lord's standards as set out in the Bible, your ascent to elevation can begin.

Now let's review some of the Lord's standards when it comes to obedience. If you're ready, go ahead and turn the page!

Chapter 3
Your Purity is a Weapon against the devil!

As we read the Bible and allow God's statues to take root in our lives, we learn that purity in a requirement, not an option.

God desires us to live clean lives. the Bible says, *Be ye holy, for I am holy.* — *1 Peter 1:16*

Please remember we are not talking about the requirements for salvation; we are reviewing God's requirements for elevation.

Salvation requires that we confess out of our mouths that Jesus is Lord. Salvation requires us to receive salvation by grace through faith, as the gift of God. — *Romans 10:9,13 and Ephesians 2:8*

Even after receiving the gift of salvation, we are called to be holy, because God is holy! Yes, the Lord expects us to sin and fall short of His glory—we all do; this is part and parcel of the human condition. If and when that happens, we

must quickly repent of the sin and begin anew.
—*Acts 3:19*

However, when seeking elevation in your life, your maturity in Christ must be at a depth that brings forth an established lifestyle of purity.

Let's look at something that will help me establish this point. One of the biggest reasons I wrote my book *Stepping Into Favor*, is because the Lord told me far too many Christians are impoverished and struggling financially in the Body of Christ, and He desires to address and remedy that.

Question: Would you agree there are many Christians who know how to quote *Philippians 4:19* but never see the manifestation thereof?

That verse says: *But my God shall supply all your need according to his riches in glory by Christ Jesus.*

Where is the disconnect?

We need to know the whole Bible rather than isolate verses that sound good, and simply call them out into the atmosphere. Some do that, get no result and then wonder later why the atmosphere isn't responding to their decrees!

Those who are truly serious about accessing God's riches in glory by Christ Jesus, will take the time to read the surrounding verses, in order to gain accurate understanding. We need to know *who* the verse is referring to, *what* it is referring to, and *how* to apply it. Continuing to establish this example for the purpose of our discussion, *Philippians 4:19* actually refers to the blessings reserved for those who bless men and women of God, specifically. People who bless leaders have access to a specific blessing provided by the Lord. Read the surrounding verses, namely verses 15-18, and see for yourself!

Therefore, correct understanding and personal command of God's Word is essential when positioning yourself to attain elevation.

Some people call for blessings they do not have legal access to. Some quote verses out of context, from a place of disobedience, then wonder why God's Word is not coming alive for them. In truth, the problem isn't with God's Word; it's with the individual!

When we have correct understanding of the Word, personal command of the Word, and begin to wield the Sword of the Spirit which is the Holy Bible from a place of obedience — ***SHAZAM!*** —

that is when you will see the atmosphere respond to your decrees and prayers! That is when you'll see elevation begin to manifest in your life!

This is why the wise King Solomon wrote, *Get wisdom, get understanding: forget it not... — Proverbs 4:5*

The Word of God is the highest authority on the planet. That's why it is referred to as the Sword of the Spirit. —*Ephesians 6:17*

But hear me: ***To wield that sword and. Have it work for you at full capacity, you must be holy.***

In *John 8:11*, we find Jesus is talking to the Samaritan woman. Jesus makes sure she understands he's not judging or condemning her, but really wants to help her. Then Jesus drops an atomic bomb: *GO, AND SIN NO MORE.*

When writing to the congregation at Thessalonica, the esteemed Apostle Paul had a lot to say on this very matter. Paul is a man we must listen to, because he had an incredible command of the Scriptures, followed by a life-changing personal encounter with Jesus Christ. His words are recorded for us, lest we stumble or begin believing false doctrine. Listen to what Paul wrote to the folks in the church of Thessalonica:

1 Thessalonians 4:1-8 — Furthermore then we beseech you, brethren, and exhort *you* by the Lord Jesus, that as ye have received of us how ye ought to walk and to please God, *so* ye would abound more and more.
    For ye know what commandments we gave you by the Lord Jesus. For this is the will of God, *even* your sanctification, that ye should abstain from fornication: That every one of you should know how to possess his vessel in sanctification and honor;
    Not in the lust of concupiscence, even as the Gentiles which know not God:
    That no *man* go beyond and defraud his brother in *any* matter: because that the Lord *is* the avenger of all such, as we also have forewarned you and testified.
    For God hath not called us unto uncleanness, but unto holiness.
    He therefore that despiseth, despiseth not man, but God, who hath also given unto us his holy Spirit.

Purity. Holiness. These are non-negotiable precursors to your elevation.

Let's conclude this chapter with *Joshua 3:5: Consecrate yourselves, for tomorrow the Lord will do amazing things among you.*

If you want to see the Lord do amazing things among you, consecrate yourself! Your purity is a weapon against the devil! Your purity is currency when pursuing elevation. Amen!

Chapter 4
FOCUS!
A vital tool for Elevation

One critical tool required as a precursor to elevation, and in order to navigate where elevation will lead you, is the ability to *focus*.

We've all heard the saying 'God doesn't give you more than you can handle.' Usually, that's spoken in reference to trials or hardships. People say, 'Well, apparently I can handle it, because God doesn't give you more than you can handle!' People also say of their hardships, 'In the name of Jesus, I'm coming out stronger!'

That's all true, and they're both very positive perspectives. In the midst of our trials, His grace *is* sufficient for us. His strength *is* made perfect in our weakness. — *2 Corinthians 12:9*
    But let's look further.
    Consider the following.

It took focus on my part, to compile the material

required for the workshop intensive that preceded this book. It took focus to subsequently write the material contained in the book you're holding. Furthermore, it took focus to create the materials my team and I used to announce and distribute this book. And, it will take focus to navigate the new blessings and responsibilities that will come as a result of releasing this book into the body of Christ.

I say all that to say this: If you want elevation and all the opportunities and blessings that come with it, you must be able to focus!

If your focus isn't so great right now, I've got good news for you! Guess what?—God can help you learn to focus! Your Father God created you; He knows your biology, psychology and physiology! He also knows you quite personally by name and down to the finite detail — He can absolutely, positively, tweak a few things here and there which will help you learn to focus! Believe that!

Back to our initial thought, how folks often say: 'God doesn't give you more than you can handle,' when referring to difficulties and trials. But do you know that saying works in the reverse, as well?

God will not give someone a blessing they can't handle! How do I know? Because in the Bible, we see Him take blessings *away from* folks who can't handle it. Such as King Saul, as we mentioned in the previous chapter.

All throughout the Bible, God gives important tasks to the people He can —*catch this*— trust with the elevation. Such as, Joseph in Potiphar's house. Daniel in Nebuchadnezzar's palace. Another great example would be Joshua and Caleb, in spying out the promised land. — *Genesis 39:5, Daniel chapters 2-6, and Numbers 13:1-2*

What we're doing now is honing in on and highlighting the need to be able to focus, receive, and navigate the landscape of your elevation. These are qualities Joseph, Daniel, Joshua, Caleb, and so many others in the Bible, had in common. Do you share that quality? If the Lord were to elevate you today, are you confident in your ability to enter that new season? Should God release a next-level assignment to you in this very hour, would you be able to focus properly and thus succeed?

This chapter is designed to motivate you to deepen your focus! The Lord is calling you to a greater capacity in the area of focus, right now! At the end of this chapter, I'm going to prophesy over you — *so get ready!*

I like to say it like this: when the Lord sees that we are 'ready containers', He then authorizes the blessing. When God sees we are able to traverse the landscape of our personal Promised Land, He then authorizes and arranges our exodus. *And a crucial quality the Lord looks for in those He is considering and preparing for elevation is the ability to focus.*

The snare of double-mindedness

A condition called double mindedness is talked about in the Bible. We will review the verses later, but for your notes, they are: *James 1:6-8.* Double mindedness is when you struggle with indecision and/or the inability to hone in, apply yourself, and follow through. To the Lord, these things introduce and often represent the presence of instability, which suggests inability.

Some may perceive that as a harsh statement, but I pray you'd much rather the Lord's prophet be honest with you than soothe you with sweet but ineffective words. My assignment is to help position you for elevation!

I'll bet you can think of someone who is indecisive. Perhaps you can think of someone who's not very good at following through, perhaps not reliable. They may be nice enough, kind enough, with very good intentions, but if you ever needed something important done, you wouldn't ask them. Why not? Because while you like them as a person, when it comes to getting an important job done or handling a blessing of value, you prefer someone you know you can rely on. Right?

Do you know anyone who is mentally unstable? Sadly, I have known people who are not in possession of their full mind. Those folks tugged at my heart strings, and I was very moved to pray for them and help them however I could as the Lord led, but it was clear they were not currently able to initiate or stick with anything — which is why sometimes those folks fail at jobs, careers, or projects.

How disturbing it is to see a person like this in a position of authority or privilege? Worse yet, how unsettling is it to see an unstable person with a public platform? Why is it disturbing, unsettling? Because there's no telling what such a person is going to do with their platform! There's no telling how they're going to use it, how they might impact or influence people, in their instability!

People with a double mind are all over the place; they're prone to mood swings, opinion changes, personality changes, even changes in spiritual and lifestyle beliefs or practices.

At the worst level, such individuals need deliverance. Other times, such individuals are simply lacking in discipline, and perhaps mental, emotional and spiritual stability, as well.

Sometimes these people wonder why they cannot elevate out of where they are. Sometimes they wonder why God has not answered their prayer or given them a blessing they asked for. Never realizing their present state of double mindedness and instability, is actually what's blocking them.

James 1:6-8 — But let him ask in faith, nothing wavering. For he that waverth is like a wave of the sea driven with the wind and tossed. For let not that man think that he shall receive any thing of the Lord. A double minded man is unstable in all his ways. (KJV)

The NLT says verse 8 like this: *Their loyalty is divided between God and the world, and they are unstable in everything they do.*

What revelation! So, our ability to focus on tasks at hand, assignments given, and our loyalty to Jesus Christ, are required for elevation. Glory to God!—what revelatory tools these are! Our God truly does desire to help position and empower us!

On A Personal Note…

The Lord spoke to me not long before writing this book, and He told me to prepare myself for a test. I had no idea what kind of a test it would be, but sure enough, the test came. Then God spoke to me again and told me to brace myself, because my pace, work-load, and schedule were all going to increase. The Lord led me to *Luke*

12:48 which says: *For unto whomsoever much is given, of him shall be much required.*

How very true that is. To whom much is given, much is required. Last year over the holidays, another minister and their family came to our home in Atlanta for Thanksgiving dinner. At the end of the evening, as we were sipping a cup of coffee while I wiped the kitchen counters and loaded the dishwasher, the minister commented, "I've barely seen you sit down since we got here." In truth, I'd sat down to eat, and I did enjoy my meal, at that! But I told that minister what I'm telling you today: *To whom much is given, much is required.*

There was a time I prayed for a husband, a home, for restoration of my family. I prayed for all my children to be healthy, and I specifically prayed to be able to entertain for holidays again, as I love to cook and extend hospitality and blessing to people. I did not receive these blessings the moment I asked for them. No, the Lord required my preparation for the elevation. You see, elevation into a godly marriage took preparation. Elevation to the position of lady of the manor in my own home, took preparation.

Elevation to the founding servant of God in a thriving ministry, took preparation. *And all that preparation, required my focus.* For to whom much is given, much is required.

Show the Lord you're ready for elevation, and He will elevate you. An excellent way to demonstrate this to the Lord, is through stewardship.

Take good care of what you have, now. Adopt a spirit and lifestyle of excellence according to *Daniel 6:3*, now. Your stewardship at this level, is the precursor to elevation. If you truly desire the Lord to shift you up a level, master your stewardship right where you are.

Excellent verses on stewardship are:
1 Peter 4:10, Matthew 25:23, and Luke 16:11.

If you're not as focused and stable as you'd like to be, let me encourage you. Again, God can help, heal, and strengthen *anyone*. He can do so for you! Go to the Lord and talk to Him about your emotions, your instability. Be honest, because He knows all the details, anyway! Tell the Lord you desire Him to help you become more focused.

The Bible gives us great hope in *Romans 12:2* where it says anyone can be transformed by the renewing of their mind.

Don't throw in the towel or give up simply because maybe you now realize, 'Wow, I've got a lot of work to do!' No, rather be encouraged! It's a journey, one you've now initiated. I'm proud of you for investing in yourself by obtaining this book! I know God is proud of you, too!

I also don't believe in coincidences. I believe everyone who reads this book, will do so on purpose. The Lord goes to great lengths to ensure the right people hear, see, and read the right things.

If you feel like the Holy Spirit is speaking to you, perhaps God knew *exactly* what He was doing, by arranging for me to speak to you through this book. He cares about you that much! He loves you that much! Talk to the Lord and be willing to allow Him to transform you by the renewing of your mind.

I can honestly tell you, just a few short years ago,

I could not have handled the pace, the demands, or even the financial bracket I'm now in. God did it. He changed me... because I submitted to Him. He will do the same for you. I'm praying for you, and standing for your success!

Let's prepare to close out this chapter by looking at *Titus 1:6-8:* An elder must be blameless, faithful to his wife, a man whose children believe and are not open to the charge of being wild and disobedient. Since an overseer manages God's household, he must be blameless--not overbearing, not quick-tempered, not given to drunkenness, not violent, not pursuing dishonest gain. Rather, he must be hospitable, one who loves what is good, who is self-controlled, upright, holy and disciplined.

These things are your goals, as you pursue and achieve personal elevation!

And now, before we move on, I feel led by the Holy Ghost to prophesy over you. Get ready!

In the name of Jesus, I declare you are growing, even now! You are growing in your mind, your emotions, and in your spirit, according to the will of God for your life as outlined in Jeremiah 29:11!

I decree and declare prophetically you are capable of wonderful things, because you are fearfully and wonderfully made! I declare you can do all things through Christ who strengthens you, and His strength is made perfect in your weakness! According to Psalm 139:14, Philippians 4:13, and 2 Corinthians 12:9!

I prophesy the Lord is about to strengthen your mind! You about to be blessed with the ability to focus! With this enhanced ability to focus, you are in preparation for personal elevation! Believe and receive that, in Jesus' name!

Chapter 5
Radical Alignment

In order to receive elevation from the Lord, you must be radically aligned with Him! You will need to cleanse yourself of the wrong relationships, influences and mindsets. You must also allow the Lord to adjust or reform existing mindsets that are damaging, destructive or hindering in nature.

I can tell you, it will be His way, or the high way! God leaves very little room for negotiation. I can also tell you this: the manifestation of His elevation in your life will be *more than you ever imagined, and so much better than anything you could have imagined, yourself!*

Radically aligning yourself with God requires dying to yourself, according to *Luke 9:23*. That verse says: *And he said to them all, If any man will come after me, let him deny himself, and take up his cross daily, and follow me.*

Jesus said: *My meat is to do the will of his that sent me, and to finish his work. — John 4:34*

You may have heard the term 'die to self' but what does that mean? It means relinquishing perspectives, habits, ideas or even goals that are not aligned with the mind and heart of the Father. It means allowing Jesus to truly be your Lord (your boss!), in addition to your Savior. It means God's will comes before your own! This way of life is a precursor to elevation from the Lord.

Colossians 3:3 — For ye are dead, and your life is hid with Christ in God.

One of my favorites: *Galatians 2:20 — I am crucified with Christ: nevertheless I live; yet not I, but Christ liveth in me: and the life which I now live in the flesh I live by the faith of the Son of God, who loved me and gave Himself for me.*

In your pursuit of elevation, which is 100% attainable for you, know that Jesus will have to come first. He will have to lead. That may mean sacrificing some ideas, goals or projects on the altar of self-interest — and to that I would say: *not every good thing is a God thing.*

Not long ago, I began a project that by all accounts, seemed like it would be very successful and quite lucrative. I encountered a few bumps and hurdles along the way, things did not align quite like I had hoped, but I'll admit I ignored the red flags. Why? Again, that project sure seemed like a potential home-run! Boy, was I in for a surprise — and a tough lesson.

Not only did the project never develop or succeed the way I'd hoped, but it ended up costing me a lot of money. As if that wasn't bad enough, the entire experience was very stressful and disappointing. I heard the Holy Spirit whisper gently: *It was a good thing... but not a God thing.* I asked why God had let me experience such a struggle. Holy Spirit replied: *Did you learn anything?*

Man oh man, did I learn a *lot.* I learned to discern good things, from God things. I learned to give my time and resources to God things, only. I learned a *lot*, and I knew the time would come when the Lord would want me to use that experience as a teaching tool, for others. That is exactly what I am doing, now.

Correct elevation comes from radical alignment with the things of God — including the projects and careers HE wants for us — not indulgence in what we believe to be good for us.

That project may have been a good one, but it did not come from the Lord. Therefore, He was not obligated to put His blessing on it. *PLEASE CATCH THE GRAVITY OF THAT.*

Proverbs 3:5-7 took on a deeper meaning: *Trust in the Lord with all your heart and do not lean on your own understanding. In all your ways acknowledge Him, and He will make your paths straight. Do not be wise in your own eyes; Fear the Lord and turn away from evil.*

The entire thing crashed and burned the week before Christmas. As I already shared, it cost me a lot of money. Did I mention I didn't have much money at that time? Yet, I had no choice but to use every penny of my holiday money, to avoid dishonor and potential debt collection. The 'partner' I'd embarked on this little project with, ran for the hills, leaving me to pay the entire debt, alone. In the spirit of transparency, I chose *not* to pursue that partner to help 'shoulder the load' because I then saw the stark differences in us.

To the dear friend reading this book, I would say this: God will allow you to fail, in order to get your attention. God will allow you to experience difficulty and even a harsh lesson, in order to teach you submission and reliance on Him. So too will the Lord allow you to engage with people who are *not* in complete and radical alignment with Him, in order to teach you to remain radically aligned with His supreme will.

My best advice to you on today? Wait on the God things; don't take the bait when the devil tempts you with good things! Use Holy Ghost discernment when considering teaming up with people; not everyone has your level of honor and integrity!

The critical lessons I learned from that experience, namely to remain radically aligned with my God, paved the way for extreme elevation, which was right around the corner! It can be the very same for you, my friend. Be encouraged!

Do not be concerned about your ability to discern good things from God things. For as you come into obedience, purity, focus, and radical alignment, you will find your ability to discern, will grow.

The greater your obedience, purity, focus and alignment, the more clearly you will hear God's voice. Other voices, sent by the enemy, can appear as an angel of light — according to *2 Corinthians 11:14*. Learn from that verse, learn from my experience!

I'll leave you with this: in *Genesis 11:1-9,* we read the interesting but cataclysmic story of the descendants of Noah who settled in the land of Shinar, a fertile land watered by the Tigris and Euphrates rivers, and there they embarked on a massive building project.

They began to build the Tower of Babel, and while it seemed like a good idea at the time, they began in a vein of disobedience, and with a wrong motive.

God had told them to be fruitful and fill the earth. That was not their focus. In fact, by the time they finished the project and the city of Babel was a thriving entity, the inhabitants were anything but obedient to the Lord.

But here is what we need to look at very carefully: *the motive.*

Genesis 11:4 — Come, let us build ourselves a city, with a tower that reaches the heavens, so that we may make a name for ourselves, otherwise we will be scattered over the face of the whole earth.

Wow! So much wrong, there. First, they began in disobedience. Then, they proceeded based on their own desires, which were rooted in fear — rather than trusting God.

Here's your take-away: Just because you *can* do something, doesn't mean you should. They had the know-how. They had the supplies. They had the resources. They had the time, they had the opportunity. *But that building project was something they were never called or instructed to do.*

Radical alignment with the will of God. Radical alignment with the heart of God. You need it. They didn't have it.

Friend, you may need to put some things on the shelf simply because they're good things, but not God things. If you want elevation from the Lord, I encourage you to come into radical alignment with the will of God!

The Bible says it is the Lord who opens doors, and closes them. — *Isaiah 22:22*

Wait on God, and if it really is a God-thing, He will let you know. He will confirm it for you, and then provide for you. When it is God's vision, He releases the provision!

At the time of writing this book, I can honestly

say I have several excellent ideas, all of which I believe I could monetize, fairly quickly. Why aren't I in active pursuit of them? I'm waiting on God. I'm waiting on His instruction to do them. Just because I *can* doesn't mean I *should,* and it is the same for you.

Elevation will come to you when God opens doors for you.
Elevation will come when you step into His plan.

Romans 12:2 reveals there are 3 levels to destiny: the acceptable, the good, and the perfect will of God. That means there are things you can do that are acceptable; there are things you can do that are good. And then there's another level: the perfect will of God.

At what point does divine elevation take place? At what level does the Lord step in and elevate you? It is debatable as to whether God has a hand in elevating you to acceptable destiny. Let us not confuse what God allows versus what He authorizes or arranges.

I don't know about you, but I've lived at levels that were perhaps 'acceptable' to God; I'm over it! I want to live far above and beyond that! I desire to elevate into the good, even the perfect will of God! How about you?!

FACT: The level of destiny to which you ascend, will be indicative of and directly related to, your obedience, purity, focus, and radical alignment with the Lord.

Keep that in mind as you go forth.

Are you ready to take another step toward personal elevation? If so, turn the page!

Chapter 6
Clarity
Learning To See Yourself
The Way God Sees You

Another critical aspect of elevation is view of self. You must *see you as Jesus sees you.*

For some of us, this is far easier said, than done. To this day, I can still recall nasty things kids said to me when I was a child. The words of a bully can replay for years and years in the mind of the person bullied, sadly keeping a person enslaved and feeling low. So too can I easily recall and recite mean and biting words my own family members have said to me and about me. If my identity was not firmly rooted in Christ, those wicked words might elevate into a word curse and effectively bind me — *CATCH THAT.*

But because I've been transformed by the renewing of my mind, no one can tell me anything different from what God says about me! And my friend, it must be the very same for you.

What your Creator says about you, is the truth. Not only is it truth, but it is the highest truth! God knows you better than anyone, because He literally designed you! God knows how many hairs you have on your head this very moment, and He knows exactly what potential and giftings He placed inside of you. *Therefore, HIS DECLARATIONS about your identity, are the highest and truest statements about who you are!*

Are you ready for a serious boost? Let's review what God says about you!

God says you are more than a conqueror!
—Romans 8:37

God says you are in line to receive an amazing inheritance, because you are co-heirs with Christ!
—Romans 8:17

God says the very same power that rose Jesus from the grave, lives inside of you! That makes you literally full of supernatural power you may not have even discovered or tapped yet! Wowza!
— Romans 6:10-11, Ephesians 1:19-20

God says you are of a royal priesthood!
—1 Peter 2:9

The Lord calls you His beloved!
— *Jeremiah 31:3*

In order to step into the elevation God has for you, you will need clarity as to your true identity. You will need to cast down every imagination that exalts itself above what God says about you. The devil is a liar and that punk *will* try to steal or hinder your elevation by leaning on old fears or insecurities. Know your enemy and approach elevation guarded, suited up in the full armor of God, armed with clarity as to your identity, and ready to soar!
Scriptural References: 2 Corinthians 10:5, John 10:10, Ephesians 6:10-18.

Your self-worth and self-view must be firmly rooted in the Word of God! Learn the scriptures used above to clarify your identity in Christ, and rely on them daily!

A word to the wise...

I wish I didn't have to say this, but you need to know there will be some who do not celebrate the elevation that will come on your life. There are sure to be people who simply do not enjoy or believe in what God is about to do for you. They may question your viability or your worth. They may question whether or not you're qualified for your elevation. Child of God, keep this in mind as you go forth: *the opinions or approval of people is not required in order for you to step into what God has for you.*

As a matter of fact, God will not be consulting any human being before elevating you. Rest assured, the Lord God will not be texting or emailing your contemporaries, peers, friends or family, to see how they feel about your breakthrough, before He does it. Jesus is not going to take a poll to make sure everyone approves of His elevating you.

No, whether or not people agree with it or support your elevation, is entirely irrelevant to God. The Lord elevates whom He chooses! God does not call ones He has deemed to be qualified, but rather He qualifies the ones He has called!

So, as you shift into elevation, do not be surprised

if some people in your current circle are simply not enthused. Pray for them! Your blessing ought to encourage them, because if God did it for you, He'll do it for them — God is no respecter of persons! — *Matthew 5:44, Acts 10:34*

You may also find that your past, checkered as it may be, has given you a very unique and oddly, a quite amazing foundation from which to elevate into your destiny. As I like to say, your history has been preparing you for destiny! You've been in prep-mode for elevation for quite some time, you just didn't know it!

Child of God, your past cannot and will not disqualify you from elevation, as long as you are blood-washed, born again, obedient to the Lord, and sold out to Jesus!

However, the correct self-view *will* be required in order for you to shift into elevation. Never forget the vital lesson we learn from *Numbers chapter 13*. In that account, some people's view of self and their latent fears, prevented them from entering into their promise. Why? They didn't believe themselves capable of meeting the challenges that came with inheritance and elevation. They didn't see themselves as God saw them.

However, *you do!* And because you see yourself as *God* sees you, you are ready for elevation! This is your time to soar!

Chapter 7
Release

As you pursue elevation, do you know in your spirit that you are ready? Wanting elevation does not mean one is *ready* for it, and one of the ways I always know someone is definitely *not ready*, is when their heart and hands are still full of last season's hurt or pain.

Let me take just a moment with this. I am not minimizing pain, and I am not discounting the very real weight of heartache. What I am definitely conveying however, is the need to be *healed*, before petitioning the Lord for elevation.

Trying to enter a new season unhealed and broken, is a recipe for disaster. The Lord desires to set you up for success, not more struggle.

I encourage you to submit to the Lord in all your ways, and let Jesus heal your heart. Give yourself the alone time with God required to move you into a position of healed and empowered.

In the spirit of transparency, I'll honestly never *forget* some of the hurtful things that were done to me. I have, however, forgiven the people involved and moved far beyond it. I did so by giving it all to the Lord.

How do you 'give it all to God'? You commit to no longer reliving the difficult or hurtful events, no longer talking about them. You realize that your thoughts have power, the power to keep you stuck in that space, because as a man thinketh in his heart, so is he. — Proverbs 23:7

You begin to edit your words, stopping yourself from complaining, gossiping, even giving voice to your hurt — because you realize your words have creative power. Which means the mere act of vocalizing what happened, over and over, can also keep you stuck. For the Bible says out of your mouth comes both blessings and curses, because your words can take form and actually impact and shape your life. — James 3:10, Proverbs 18:21

Therefore, you have chosen to move on. It doesn't mean you have forgotten, but you have definitely forgiven. It doesn't mean you don't remember, but you have definitely chosen to now make new memories.

It doesn't mean you no longer have a past, it simply means you have released the past and are ready to invest your focus and heart, in a new future with Jesus.

When you are in that space, guess what? You have given it —*whatever 'it' is*— to God. Now God can work with your heart. Now the Lord can begin to heal you and prepare you for elevation. You have given yourself over to Lord Jesus. Hallelujah!

Maybe you're not there, yet. I would ask you: Do you want to be? Why don't you commit to releasing the past, today? Commit to release, in the name of Jesus! Doing so will immediately put you on a better path.

Some people have ungodly soul ties. This too can hinder elevation. Such a soul tie can prevent you from progressing. An ungodly soul tie can prevent you from elevating. How so? Again, it is impossible to receive something *new* if your hands, head, heart (or all three!) are already full of something *old*.

Release today, my friend. Give it all to God. The Lord wants to give you His best. The Lord wants to shift you into a place of renewal and empowerment. Release… so you can receive.

I encourage you to be willing to walk away from the wrong things, so God can give you the right things. That's what I had to do six years ago, and it was a truly difficult thing. But I have never regretted doing so, even though the journey took effort.

Release. I did, you can too.
Let go of the past… Jesus is calling you to a new future. Let go of the old… the Lord has something new for you.

Chapter 8
Commitment

In order to position yourself for elevation, you must be committed to the future. Namely, *God's version* of your future, which may mean relinquishing your own version.

Some people will stay where they are, in order to do things their own way. Some people will stay where they are, in order to avoid doing something they're afraid to do, or simply don't want to do.

And some people will remain where they are, even though it is clear things are *not* working optimally, because they refuse to acknowledge they made a mistake, or need help.

If any of those categories of people sounds like you, I encourage you to take on a spirit of humility, now. It is far better to admit you were wrong or that you misjudged a situation or opportunity, rather than to miss out on a God ordained opportunity.

Be committed to getting the victory, even if it means waiting on the Lord's timing. Commit to getting the victory even if it means doing some much-needed inner work!

My friend, I encourage you to be so committed to stepping into God's plan for your future, that you are willing to bring yourself into alignment with the will of God!

A strong relationship with Jesus is critical now and as you shift into elevation. This takes commitment and maintenance! Join me in making daily prayer, praise and worship, as well as Bible study, a part of your routine. Yes, every day! That is how we stay strong in the Lord.

If God points out something wrong or something He wishes you to change, be humble and allow Him to correct you. Better to course correct yourself now, then suffer later, knowing you missed out on elevation.

Matthew 5:5 says the meek or the humble, will inherit the earth, therefore they are blessed. Be humble, allow the Lord to mold and prepare you! Inheritance will be your reward!

2 Chronicles 7:14 says: *If My people who are called by My name will humble themselves, and pray and seek My face and turn from their wicked ways, then I will hear from heaven and will forgive their sin and heal their land.*

Psalm 25:9 says: *He leads the humble in what is right, and teaches the humble His way.*

1 Peter 5:5 says: *Clothe yourselves, all of you, with humility toward one another, for God opposes the proud but gives grace to the humble.*

And that also works the other way around. Listen to *Psalm 55:19 — God will give ear and humble them, He who is enthroned from of old, Selah - because they do not change and do not fear God.*

Humility, a commitment to remaining humble, and a commitment to see through what you started — these qualities must be present as you prepare for elevation. We learn the power of commitment, integrity, and seeing things through from King David. David was a finisher! Meaning, he began many things, and he finished them.

The Lord knew He could count on David. When it came to handing out assignments, God knew David was reliable, because David was committed. What an excellent example we have in King David!

When the Lord shifts you into elevation, He will expect you to be committed at whatever He calls you to. Perhaps God is going to give you a business, a project, a movement, or platform to steward. In each of those scenarios, the Lord will expect you to be committed. Having all other components in place: obedience, purity, focus, radical alignment, clarity and release — will help you to do so.

Take a moment and consider the truth of the following statement: *As a born again, blood-washed, faithful follower of Jesus Christ, having concluded this book, you now have the revelation and instruction required, to position yourself for next-level elevation. God is speaking to you. He is saying:* IT'S YOUR TIME TO SOAR!

In Conclusion

*Closing Thoughts from
Prophet JoLynne*

I believe you have what it takes to shift into elevation, otherwise the Lord would not have led you to obtain this book. As I stated in an earlier chapter, I do not believe in coincidences with the Lord!

I also believe I will hear many reports of elevation in the body of Christ, that come directly as a result of this book. I pray fervently yours is one of them!

If you embrace everything God spoke through the pages of this book and much more importantly, through the verses we quoted from the Holy Bible, then you will step into position for elevation!

Friend, this is your time to soar! Be bold and say it out loud: It's my time to soar!

As I concluded the writing of this material, I heard the voice of the Lord say chains would fall as a result of the anointing released through this book! Therefore, I encourage to share this book with others. It's time for the body of Christ to step into favor, shift into position, elevate, and soar! Glory to God!

I see prophetically that people will come out of hiding after reading this book. They've been hiding behind excuses, hiding behind fear, hiding behind hesitation or procrastination — but not anymore! The season just changed — it's your time to soar!

Chains are falling off right now! Perhaps you have been hiding behind expired plans, obstacles of your own making. Now you will get into position for rapid elevation! I speak acceleration over you in the name of Jesus!

My prayers are with you as you go forth. In the mighty and matchless name of Jesus, I declare you are coming into your season, your time to soar! This *is* your time for elevation, in Jesus' name!

May the Lord bless and guide you abundantly, in Jesus' name! May the Holy Spirit speak to you clearly, in Jesus' name! May angels encamp around you as you step into your elevation and all the experiences that will come as a result of it! And my friend, may your whole life be saturated with the goodness of God, unleashed and manifested through the wonder-working power of the Blood of Jesus!

I'm praying for you!
I'm believing for your success!
God bless you!

- Prophet JoLynne Whittaker

Are you ready to live in the favor of God as your lifestyle?

A gift from JoLynne

Stepping into the favor of God changed my life and marriage, exponentially! Favor as a lifestyle is truly something that cannot be explained, it must be experienced!

I always believed in the Lord's favor and what it could mean for my life, but as I read the Bible and examined the experiences of King David, for example, I became more and more determined to access the Lord's timeless blessings and favor as my *lifestyle* just the way David did.

Guess what? I did it, and you can too. If you have never read my best-selling book, Stepping Into Favor, I have included a powerful excerpt on the next few pages, simply to bless you.

Since stepping into favor, my life has never been the same, and I want you to experience the same blessing! Grab your Bible and a grab a notebook too if you like, and let's do a little work together! I seriously want to help you experience God's favor in a new way, on another level.

Why am I so driven to do so? Well, as I said, I am a former underdog. I understand all too well the ramifications of a poverty and a lifetime of financial struggle. Furthermore, helping Christians to prosper is a vital part of my current assignment as a prophet of the Lord!

God desires to establish you financially and hence empower and free you from financial bondages. The Lord desires all His faithful children to access His riches in glory through Christ Jesus *(Philippians 4:19)*! So if you're ready, turn the page and let's get started!

- JOLYNNE WHITTAKER

STEPPING *into* FAVOR

ACCESS GOD'S TIMELESS BLESSINGS

An excerpt from
Chapter 3
of
STEPPING INTO FAVOR

Prosperity — Of God Or Not?

(A few bad apples gave Prosperity a bad name...)

Throughout the Bible, we see God's clear and consistent style of blessing: The Lord blesses His faithful and obedient children with land, homes, resources, health, wealth, and the acumen required to cultivate or acquire such things.

Both stability and abundance are important to God. He desires for you to be secure, yet He also desires for you to be in a position to aid and bless others. Jehovah Jireh is the God of provision, but He is also the God of abundant overflow. - *Genesis 22:14, Malachi 3:10*

Allow me to say with Holy Ghost infused boldness and confidence: wealth, generational promises of wellbeing and prosperity, financial stability and overflow — *all these things are of God.*

Again, favor from a secular source may come with strings attached. You may find yourself owing someone a favor in return, if they extend a favor to you.

Or, you may find yourself indebted to that individual, now at their mercy or under their control.

Godly favor is not contaminated by such debased and sinful demands.

Your Bible says God wants you to prosper, He wants you to succeed. He has only well-wishes for you. The Lord does not desire His loyal and faithful children to suffer, struggle, or go without. - *Jeremiah 29:11*

Poverty breeds a pervasive atmosphere of desperation and fear. I should know, I grew up in poverty, surrounded by other impoverished people. Poverty isn't pretty, nor does it breed pretty behaviors.

The desperation that comes with an ongoing impoverished lifestyle causes people to act irrationally. That same desperation, fueled by a lack of finances, often drives people to do things that are erratic, dangerous, uncharacteristic of their normal behavior — just to provide for their needs.

This is the exact opposite of God's plan for the environ of your mind and atmosphere of your home.

Poverty causes one to live in fear, because it robs you of your stability, confidence, freedom and empowerment.

I recall how instability and fear pervaded the neighborhood in which I grew up. This is in contrast with God's wish for us. *2 Timothy 1:7 says: For God has not given us the spirit of fear; but of power, and of love, and of a sound mind.*

Poverty or financial disadvantage causes the absence of basic human provision: food, someplace to call 'home', a spirit that is calm and at peace. The absence of these things is where the fear comes from. There is no peace, because there's simply too much instability.

John 14:27 says: Peace I leave with you, My peace I give you; not as the world gives do I give to you. Let not your heart be troubled, neither let it be afraid.

Philippians 4:6-7 says: Be anxious for nothing, but in everything by prayer and supplication, with thanksgiving, let your requests be made known to God; and the peace of God, which surpasses all understanding, will guard your hearts and minds through Christ Jesus.

*Poverty is the devil's wish for you.
Prosperity is God's wish for you.
Which do you prefer?*

My friend, financial struggle, fear, poverty and lack are products of Satan's world, not God's.

The Word of God makes this clear. God's Word also makes it clear that under Satan's system, our peace and provision will be attacked. -John 10:10

Therefore, the Lord has created provision: His favor.
Glory to God!

We learn from the stunning and utterly breathtaking structure of the garden of Eden, exactly what God intended for us: abundance, provision, enjoyment, a life lacking nothing.

The garden of Eden was beautiful! The garden was loaded with good things to eat! Adam and Eve wanted for nothing! They had animals for companionship and entertainment. Any food they craved to satisfy a savory or sweet tooth, was literally at their fingertips.
No stress. No worry. No fear. No lack. No wondering where they were going to live, what uncertainties tomorrow would bring, what they were going to eat, or how they were going to pay for it.

That, my friends, is God's wish, His way.
Under the Lord's rule and leadership, we have what we need, and more.
Please begin to associate abundance with God.
Please begin to associate overflow with God.
Please begin to associate a life of plenty and so much more than enough, with God.
Because life and life more abundantly are exactly what Jesus came to give us, as that is God's way! Abundance is the Lord's style! - *John 10:10, Philippians 4:19*

Prosperity from the Lord provides above and beyond all we need and ask, because God desires to see us in possession of overflow — so we can give and live freely, with ease. - *Ephesians 3:20*

Are you catching on yet, that prosperity from the Lord means you are completely well, safe, abundant and blessed?

Are you seeing from God's perspective, that His brand of prosperity means you are well equipped to deal with anything and everything that comes your way, because you are stable, secure and equipped?

Christian, God's prosperity which includes His favor, empowers you in a unique and supernatural way.

Prosperity from the Lord is linked to being so self-sufficient that we have no lack, because nothing is missing! All our needs are met, and then some.

Prosperity from the Lord is linked to a personality and attitude that is pleasant and agreeable. And understandably so, because when your needs are met and you want for nothing, you enter in rest and joy!

Even in moments of temporary challenge or seeming difficulty, the joy remains because confidence in God's favor tells us breakthrough is on the way!

As you go forth, reading and integrating the teachings in this book, I urge you to be in constant prayer that the Lord prepare you to receive His favor.

Pray the Lord prepares you to be a ready container for His prosperity.

Pray the Lord adjusts anything in you that needs adjusting and reveals anything you need to do on your end, so you can step into His favor.

Pray to have the faith, boldness, and readiness to step into God's magnificent and life-changing favor with a strong heart, a clear mind, and a right spirit!

My strong admonition to you is this, dear reader: keep your relationship with the Lord strong, and your humility high.

Keep your eyes ever focused on Christ!
As you commit more fully than you ever have to this Christian walk, you will go deeper into your relationship with the Lord and begin to encounter His precious gift of prosperity.
For the favor of God is truly a natural by-product of being a ready container who is in good standing with Him!

The responsibility will be yours to remember that this world is passing away. Your goal is to attain heaven. We are to store up treasures in heaven, not here on earth. *- Matthew 6:20*

The current assignment of the Church is to preach the gospel in preparation for the return of Jesus Christ, even as the Kingdom of God is made manifest.

Anything you receive or enjoy in the meantime, is temporary and must be regarded as such.

With this knowledge firmly in place, you will be ready to step into the favor of God!
For this is your Heavenly Father's provision and blessing for you, even as you await the return of our beloved Lord and Savior, Christ Jesus!

The favor of God is your *gift to enjoy...* in the meantime.

    Are you ready?
    Let me help you get in position to step into favor!

I hope you enjoyed that excerpt. If you would like to read the whole book, you may order your own copy of Stepping Into Favor at:
www.JoLynneWhittaker.org
    (or)
www.SteppingIntoFavor.com

Are you following JoLynne Whittaker Ministries on social media?

Join the prophet on the following platforms:

Facebook | Instagram | Twitter
YouTube | Periscope